THE
Goddess League

ANASHAY GOULD

WWW.13THANDJOAN.COM

The Goddess League. Copyright 2018 by Anashay Gould.

All rights reserved. No part of this publication may be reproduced, distributed, or transmitted in any form or by any means, including photocopying, recording, or other electronic or mechanical methods, without the prior written permission of the publisher, except in the case of brief quotations embodied in critical reviews and certain other noncommercial uses permitted by copyright law. For permission requests, write to the publisher, addressed "Attention: Permissions Coordinator," 500 N. Michigan Avenue, Suite #600, Chicago, IL 60611.

13th & Joan books may be purchased for educational, business or sales promotional use. For information, please email the Sales Department at sales@13thandjoan.com.

Printed in the U.S. A.

First Printing, January 2019

Library of Congress Cataloging-in-Publication Data has been applied for.

ISBN 978-1-7326464-4-5

Dedication

THIS BOOK IS dedicated to my younger self, an awkward tall girl, who wanted the knowledge gleaned in the pages of this book and who sought solutions for inspiration and empowerment. The solutions that I speak of could not be found because there weren't any. There was a lack of information and there weren't any books to reference. I was at a loss when in search of ways to ease my discomfort while being tall. Now, I can only hope to bridge that gap and to provide insight to young ladies that are considered *too tall for their age*.

To My Goddess Readers,

I WOULD LIKE TO first take the time and thank each and every one of you for purchasing my book. My book has been a labor of love, and it was birthed because I always felt so misunderstood. I never quite felt I was from this planet, and it didn't help that I stood well above my peers at six feet four inches tall.

I remember feeling forgotten at one time in my life. Not forgotten in the traditional sense, but I felt as if the world didn't have women who looked like me, thought like me or had similar interests. I felt like I was forgotten because I lived in the middle of nowhere. Who was thinking about me enough to express my innermost feelings? I didn't like feeling forgotten, but I wasn't quite sure what to do about it. I just knew I didn't want others, like me, to experience what I was going through–alone and forgotten.

I wrote this book because I want to tell you that I was in desperate need of help as a teenager. I didn't have the guidance for which I yearned and needed, but never found. I hope my story will enlighten and empower younger and older women. My desire is to provide a tangible reference for anyone who has ever felt forgotten or is presently feeling forgotten. All you have to do is pick up my book and know that there is someone in this world who has experienced feeling alone and forgotten and remembers you. Not only do I remember you, but I SEE you. I see you for all the struggles and complexities that make up your day to day lives. It is very possible that I can relate to you in some way or another.

I can only wish that I had had this knowledge unlocked to me during my teenage years, but I am thankful to be used as a vessel to promote love and compassion for generations to come.

Peace and Light,
Anashay

Acknowledgements

To MY FRIENDS and family: Thank you for your everlasting support. I love you guys.

TO SCOTT: THANK you for pouring love into me daily. I love you to the moon and back!

INTRODUCTION
WHAT IS A GODDESS?

A GODDESS IS A woman who flows through life and possesses the ability to be patient while maintaining balance. She is constantly evolving while managing a healthy harmony of mind, body and spirit. A Goddess is a woman with an intangible aura, magnified by her sense of self-awareness and her love of life. She has the gift of communicating through her actions, and she is inspiring and influencing because she has confidence in abundance. She has a zest for life that permits her to be free from the grasp of society and filled with compassion, peace, fun and joy. A Goddess strives for love and understanding that are enveloped in personal growth and the knowledge that life is what she makes it.

WHAT IS THE PURPOSE OF THE GODDESS LEAGUE?

I WANTED TO create stories of those with similar backgrounds and give them a place to lift their voice, share their most intimate details and express challenges they may think they deal with in isolation. I am hopeful that this book will ultimately give birth to a community of individuals uniting on everyday topics that could only be understood by "tall" girls. My purpose is to provide a platform for young ladies and women who yearn for a cohesive group that can not only relate to each other, but also provide guidance and gradual solutions. Gradual solutions imply being patient as solutions may be discovered gradually over time. Upholding a sense of solitude and understanding and refraining from being judgmental will be highly valued.

We must break down all barriers and face the issues that we think we have overcome. This book is a "call to action" for us to address the repetition of the vicious cycle of self-doubt that results in isolation or deflated confidence. I say no more! You are worthy; you are beautiful, and I want to be a constant reminder of this fact every time you read the words on these pages.

When you explore the world around you, I can only hope that you pay it forward and uplift someone who seems to be going through what you know to be an obstacle. It is so important to have a guide and/or a mentor to trust and who can assist you with easing deterrents. Bearing the weight of so many insecurities can be damaging to one's mentality. I value one's frame of mind and encourage each of us to stand tall in the face of adversity. We must love our being throughout our entire existence. I will never tire of being supportive, and this is a declaration I won't get tired of making. To simply explain it: Goddess represents vast power with undeniable presence and beauty. The goal of *The Goddess League* collectively is to spread love, acceptance and guidance to those that we would have the privilege to educate. With this vision, let me be the first to introduce myself and provide a little insight on ways that I was able to overcome my obstacles and some of the lessons that I have learned along the way. I can only hope that I empower you into the action of sharing your experiences. After all, this is a league of OUR stories.

THE GODDESS LEAGUE

HERE'S WHAT TO EXPECT

IN THESE NEXT few chapters, I would like to explain, in detail, the characteristics of a Goddess. I have told you what a Goddess represents; now, I want to get into the how of achieving such a title. When a Goddess flows through life, she possesses the ability to be patient with those around her throughout

THE PROCESS OF learning to know, accept and love herself on all levels. You will read about this ability and find it addressed in the chapter: Challenge of Acceptance. The Mind chapter talks about the permission to be free from the grasp of society and being filled with the knowledge that life is what you make it. The Body chapter talks about a woman with an intangible, something you can't touch (but you know it exists), aura that is magnified by her sense of self-awareness and body language. Last, but not least, the Harmony chapter touches on communication through actions that aspire to influence. Throughout this book, you will feel waves of confidence will sweep over you. Amidst an enlightened mentality, I hope that you will discover a newness within and be empowered to own all that you are. It is my greatest desire to ensure that you

feel great about the height that God has blessed you to have.

TABLE OF CONTENTS

ACKNOWLEDGMENTS VII
INTRODUCTION IX

CHAPTER 1: Challenge of Acceptance:
You are Tall, Embrace It 1
CHAPTER 2: The Mind 11
CHAPTER 3: The Body 21
CHAPTER 4: Harmony 37
EPILOGUE 47

ABOUT THE AUTHOR 49
CONNECT WITH THE AUTHOR 51

THE GODDESS LEAGUE

1

CHALLENGE OF ACCEPTANCE: YOU ARE TALL, EMBRACE IT.

MY NAME IS Anashay Gould. I stand proudly and dignified at six feet, four inches and I am a Goddess. I absolutely love me! I have accomplished being who I am through the process of learning, accepting and loving myself on all levels. I am a nurturer by trade and I practice the art of compassion daily.

My credentials of being a Certified Personal Life Coach and a natural enthusiast, offer a glimpse of who I am. I appeared on American Idol when I was aspiring to be a singer, and I also served as a soldier in the United States Air Force. I was a model who graced runways and the pages of magazines, not to mention my very own magazine cover, which was the highlight of my very short career! I have been fortunate enough to be an ambassador of many causes and I have had opportunities to carry out my dreams. My desire is to be a doer and not a wisher. I like to think that I attract good things, because I am a good person. I find humility in naming all of the things that I have done, and I present them to offer hope that you can be all that you desire.

Although I am a qualified professional in reference to life coaching, I am in no way promoting this book as an example of how a life coaching session works. It should in no way be compared because this book is completely different from an individual session. I only wanted to state a title that I have been trained on as well as provide insight as to what type of person I am and what I am all about. Let me be clear: I am not telling you what to do, but I am presenting the following text that is full of suggestions and struggles that I have personally faced, being a woman of height.

Did you know that a belief is nothing more than a thought that we repeat over and over? Have you ever stopped to realize that every decision we make is based on that belief system? Whether we hear the message from our own minds or through the repetition of others, a belief is formed. Accepting who we are can't be achieved alone, it usually results from seeing others who serve as a resemblance of who we are or who we desire to be. We often hear stories and experiences that we can relate to, and we acquire the permission to accept ourselves. When you accept who you are, it will result in growth. Some people call it change, but I beg to differ. When you are growing, you are steadily moving in one direction as opposed to change which simply means a turn-around.

I remember being six years old and getting compared to trees and bean poles. I am thankful that no one ever made fun of me, but I was still self-conscious because I stood a foot taller than the rest of my peers. I was long, tall and lanky…no wonder everyone thought I was older than I looked! Although I didn't behave as someone older, I was still faced with that stigma. I really felt alone in those moments, because I just felt like no one could understand what I was going through. I didn't know how to go about changing it, and it bothered me to no end. You know how most of us wanted to hurry and become an adult? Well, that wasn't the case for me. It bothered me that people associated my height with my age, because I would always think: now I know good and well my face doesn't look that old! I wasn't allowed to wear makeup for my entire childhood and teen years. I was also wearing prescription glasses by fourth grade. To me, I resembled a nerd. In all honesty, I was most definitely a nerd, and I can say that with pride now! I took offense to being seen and considered as an older person.

Thankfully, I could share some of my frustration with my sisters who had already experienced some of these things, and they could relate. Don't get me wrong, I didn't go to them for every little thing. I am the baby of seven brothers and sisters, and we are a family I affectionately call Goliaths. I was fortunate enough to never get picked on due to my predecessors being part of the "cool kids." I grew up in a town that had a total population of thirteen hundred people, and everyone was much like family, so you were treated with love and kindness.

I grew up in a predominately white town, so a sense of identity was a fleeting mission. I love the little town I came from, and I know that it played a huge part in shaping my life. At the time, I didn't really know who I wanted to be. However, I think I already knew what type of person I wanted to be. I had no clue about the journey it would take to arrive there. I am a firm believer that acquiring a sense of oneself is achieved through the cultivation of experiences that sculpts us into an individual existence. Let me say that again: To acquire a sense of oneself is achieved through the cultivation of experiences that sculpts us into an individual existence. I know that is a lot to take in! Please let me further explain. To obtain your identity, you can reach success through the development of life and its experiences. That in turn molds or shapes you to lead a life that was ESPECIALLY created for you throughout your existence.

In my case, I had living, breathing visuals, my siblings, that I could duplicate. My ultimate persona was comprised from who I am and alternate versions of those that surrounded me. I acquired the good traits from the people I aspired to be and from those around me, and I molded them to fit my personality.

That opportunity can be afforded to all of us if only we would stop trying to compete and compare ourselves to others and learn the practice of altering our thoughts to evolve. Instead of viewing others as threatening, we must learn to use them as motivation. Your journey is yours and yours alone. Your competing or comparing yourself won't do you any good; however, if you feel disappointed in your own actions, it can only mean that you know better. Coming to that conclusion, can lead to affirmative action in your quest for acceptance of self. We are ever evolving, and you should know that it is natural and encouraged. My mantra is: *All lessons are learned through mistakes; therefore, you should embrace all that you are and love yourself through all imperfections.* I wished I looked like my peers, but I learned that God doesn't make mistakes. I even wished to be someone else and be from somewhere else, but it was not meant to be.

I was in the middle of nowhere, and sometimes I felt so misunderstood. I knew that I was different, and that made me sick, because I didn't want to be different. God had made me this way, so I had to embrace it. I knew my mind worked on a different frequency than most. I was constantly putting myself in others' shoes just so I could try and understand where they were coming from. I have always felt so compassionate and empathetic to everyone and about everything! I am sure it had much to do with reading fictional novels…I kept my nose in a book. I loved being swept away to another time or some alternate universe; anything was better than my drab life! I like to believe that reading allowed me to extend my thoughts. Some books would stir emotions and ideas I wasn't aware of. I always wanted more… more knowledge, more adventures, more characters. I was so curious about life and inquisitive about what else the world had to offer and what else I could explore. Journaling was another passion for me, because it promoted my muscle memory. My mind remains what I am most proud of. I was an overachiever in all things academic.

I was thankful that I went to a small school, because our curriculum was more advanced, which allowed me to keep my mind sharp. Unfortunately, I moved away to a larger school, and the unthinkable happened. I got "dumber", and this is a true statement! Apparently, I was six months ahead of the freshman class; therefore, I had to wait until we were on the same level of education. I was forced to sit through and listen to what I already knew. The pace was so much slower, and I didn't find myself being challenged as much. My need to try dissipated. I still managed to graduate in the top ten percent of my class, but due to my Mom being ill, I never pursued some of the academic scholarships that were presented to me as I wanted to stay close to home. I didn't receive any athletic scholarships, and I was not at all surprised! I am sure that stems back to my feeling awkward. My body was my enemy, and I managed to put it through the ringer. I have the bruises and scars to prove it! There wasn't a wall, corner or door that I didn't manage to run into…ugh! I can also admit that I was a terrible athlete. I started playing basketball when I was about eight years old, and I played until I was sixteen, but I remember thinking that I didn't want to play. It just wasn't what I wanted to do. I used to feel forgotten or left out, because all of the representation I was seeing for girls my height were basketball players or models. Who was out there that represented me and all of the other things that could potentially interest me? Better yet, why had I never met them or heard of them? Those were the moments I truly felt the most misunderstood. As I continued to grow like a weed, everyone expected me to be coordinated, but to my embarrassment and frustration, I was FAR from it. I hardly wanted to move for fear that I would knock something over, or even worse, my endless limbs would whack somebody in the face! I know people were tired of me always apologizing, and most of them would keep a safe distance away after they learned the hard way not to get too close. I can smirk now because it's funny. Today, I can't get people to give me space. It definitely wasn't funny back then! I was constantly tripping over my own two feet, and as my Mom would say, I couldn't walk and chew bubble gum at the same time. Thank God for growth.

Let me also mention that I grew up only being permitted to wear skirts and dresses. Finding clothes that didn't look like they were costuming for *Little House on the Prairie*, an old TV show back in the 70's, was a *no go*. And, no, I didn't watch the show. It was just a reference! Somehow, some way, I managed to look fashionable enough as my Mom was a seamstress, but the struggle was real. I used to hate the fact that I couldn't wear shorts during the summer. I had to wear skirts for all of my sporting events, but that, my friends, is another topic—one I won't get into!

I was fortunate enough to grow up around good, loving, country folk. In that regard, you may ask yourself what hardships could I have possibly faced? In my case, they weren't necessarily on the surface but moreso in my mind. If you don't know, the mind is where one's truest reality lies. On the surface, I appeared to be figuring it out, but that was far from the truth. I didn't divulge or share many thoughts or issues with my family because I didn't want to come across as the little sister with petty worries. Of course, that is not how they would have received me, but it was all in my mind. My Mother was not someone whom I felt would understand, so I didn't share most of my thoughts with her. Now, if I would've had someone like a mentor, I think I would have allowed myself to be more open and honest about my inner turmoil. I remember thinking: Were other girls like me going through this? If they were, I had no idea, because that particular message was never conveyed or brought to my attention. When I think about my younger self, fueled with a desire to seek out answers only to find none, my message was born. I wanted to make certain that women of height whom I crossed paths with would be aware of my message. My desire is to shower women of height with love, help them to acquire confidence, and to spread acceptance to all who may feel misunderstood. I am a nurturer by trade and I want to extend affirmations and confidence to you.

This brings me full circle as to why this League is so important. Sometimes, it is easier to know you won't be judged or frowned upon for the smallest issues or doubts, because someone else has gone through the exact same thing. You don't have to be embarrassed or second guess yourself, because there is now a platform for you from which to speak and receive sound advice. This sentiment can help to reiterate you are not alone.

THE GODDESS LEAGUE

2

THE MIND

THEY SAY THE mind is a terrible thing to waste, and I completely concur. Your mind is a muscle that can be trained to become stronger, and it can be trained in a multitude of ways. I want to provide some insight and give some tools on how to do just that.

Let us begin by looking in the mirror and saying something nice about ourselves. This is a practice called affirmation. I was shocked when I realized just how few people do this and how even fewer have actually ever heard of it. It is a simple routine that can be done when you get up in the morning. You might say, *I love me*, or *I am going to have a great day*. Keep it simple if it's your first time and don't overthink it, because there is honestly no right or wrong way. If you want an alternative method, feel free to look up a quote on the internet that resonates with you and write it on a sticky note and post it on your mirror. I just want you to start right away because once you do, you will steadily start to see the difference in your life. Be creative and post sticky notes on your alarm clock, headboard, in your closet or in any space you tend to visit often. It's just a healthy reminder that you are awesome! You should be aware that words have power and saying something nice about yourself preceding the start of your day will ignite more favorable outcomes. You are great; you are mighty, and you were blessed with your height for a purpose. Don't be so hard on yourself, because we can be our toughest critics. Progression is change that can only be fueled by your desire to behave and perform differently. Continue to evolve while maintaining consistency in all you say or do and watch it pay off abundantly. When you project an inner confidence and peace, you will attract the same type of energy.

I wanted to touch briefly on meditation because it is instrumental in centering your state of mind. It allows you to handle situations with ease while reducing stress. This act involves self-awareness and promotes the focal point of quieting your mind and becoming more connected to those around you. In case you are not familiar, let me provide an overview of the steps you can take for meditation:

- Choose a peaceful location.

- Wearing comfortable clothing is recommended.
- Breathe at a steady rate.
- Clear the mind and fill it with thoughts of peace.
- Sitting with crossed legs is recommended.
- Try and meditate for five minutes at the same time each day.

Again, mediating is just the act of clearing one's mind and eliciting serenity. If you find yourself distracted during meditation, don't be so hard on yourself, everything becomes easier over time. I recently started this practice myself, and though I was doubtful, I tried it anyway. I am a better person for it! The goal is to retain peaceful energy throughout your day. These practices mentioned will help you sustain an identity and build a solid foundation for your frame of mind. It is completely up to you to harness and preserve that delicate balance of not falling back into old habits. Those habits can consist of letting your day start off negatively, not doing anything to dispel or get rid of such energy, or letting your emotions get the best of you. I implore you to visualize beyond your current line of sight so that you can delve into how you are perceived versus how you want to be perceived.

Based on my stature alone, people concluded that I was someone who was intimidating and that I used this as an advantage over others. Automatically, I was made out to be aggressive, which was totally unfair and far from the truth! I kept finding myself wanting to bend over backwards to make everyone else comfortable. Some people used to say I could make a living being a comedian; I was so funny! In retrospect, I believe I was only that silly to put people at ease. I found humor to be an icebreaker, and I hated when people acted awkwardly around me. I wanted to scream, "just be yourself!" I realized that I made it my purpose for them to feel comfortable enough to do just that. I was always the one asked to pose in the back of a group photo. I was always the one asked to squat down as not to make others feel so short. I was always the one taming my tongue, because I knew if I caused conflict I would only add credibility to the unjust picture some had already painted of me. I felt like I was trying so much harder than everyone else, and sometimes I did let that get the best of me. I am only human right? I have a word of advice—Keep a cool head when dealing with people, because some of them may try to provoke you to get a rise out of you. You can either take the bait, or you can literally be the bigger person. When addressing someone, choose your words wisely, and if possible with a smile. My smile came after many failed attempts on my part, so don't think you will master this overnight. Remember the meditation steps that I mentioned earlier? Well, this is a time when remaining calm is needed. Never allow anyone to steal your vibes, because you will have your mind all the way together!

I am a *glass half full* type of woman. I like to think I listen and try to understand where someone is coming from. I felt the need to do that, because I wanted to be admitted the same courtesy. My positive outlook on situations doesn't allow much to keep me down, this includes people for that matter. I remain encouraging and supportive, because I take the time to center myself through affirmations and meditation. This also had much to do with conditioning my mind to think first and react second. I wasn't aggressive nor confrontational by nature, but I always made sure I spoke my mind. Understand that being assertive or direct is necessary, and you should never be afraid to ask or let your desires be known. People aren't going to be able to figure that out for you, and you shouldn't expect them to automatically know. My words and thoughts were coming from such a genuine place that people started to respect my honesty and directness. I felt empowered and liberated because the more I expressed myself, the more comfortable I became. When you are able to clearly get your message across, people will remember and appreciate you. It has the tendency to build better relationships, create fewer misunderstandings, and you could be rewarded with new opportunities. Keep in mind the delivery in which you speak is very important. Leaving people with an influential aura of positivity, doused with a tinge of truthfulness, can leave a lasting impression…for the better.

Living for the approval of others is something you should not do, but I know that is easier said than done. I was a victim of that myself. Yet, I am way too independent and way too dominant to let those people, the ones I did and did not know, keep me from my truth. Keep in mind this can be acquired through knowing your self-worth and loving yourself no matter what. The process of learning and being able to accept and love yourself on all levels is the direction to take.

    This brings me to being mindful of the company you keep. You must be at peace and enjoy your own company before you start seeking out others. I say that to say this: we can be impressionable, even past our teen years. If you are not sure and solid in who you are, then that is when we let in the naysayers and those alike. They say two brains are better than one, but I can tell you if the two are not on one accord, it can be detrimental to your foundation, especially if it wasn't built in cement. You will start to take on their traits and ways, and who you are can become overshadowed. Find a circle of people who love you enough to tell you the truth. I can't iterate this enough. Everyone faces fear, doubts and screw-ups, and the faster you become at acknowledging this truth, the faster you will flourish. I repeat, don't be so hard on yourself and embrace the changes. Getting comfortable with who you are unleashes boundless possibilities for your personal growth. We, the tall Goddesses, were not designed to simply fit in but to be unyielding, bold and proud.

Gifted with height can come with great responsibility and courage. We were afforded a gem, and to look at it any other way is unacceptable! Unknowingly, we can be placed on a natural platform that demands attention, and some of us may not know what to do with it. I say why not do something positive and spread a little cheer? If you think no one is paying attention, you couldn't be more wrong. Give someone a hug, a smile or a kind gesture. If people are going to watch, you may as well set a good example! It may even initiate them to extend the same courtesy. Keep doing you, because you never know who is watching and whose life you might illuminate. My friends and family would get so annoyed when people would make the statement, "Wow, you are so tall!" I never knew whether to say "thank you" or "duh"! I would also respond: "Yes, I know that" as I am giving them the side eye. However, light was shed on what they were really trying to say. I started to take it as "Wow, you are beautiful!" At least, that's the interpretation I was choosing to go with just to keep my own sanity! Some people are not good at giving compliments, in fear of offending someone, so they only state facts. When I looked at it from that angle, my mood improved significantly and so did my demeanor. People feel as though they have a right to stare at us and make comments simply because they don't feel like we should take offense. That may be the case, but it can still come off as rude. Half of them don't mean it that way. Once I learned to look at it from a brighter perspective and embraced my fabulousness, I took everything as a compliment whether it was meant that way or not! Honey, they could compare me to a horse, and I would think to myself, thank ya, thank ya, kindly! I am not saying they did, but I am just giving you an example of how unbothered I was, lol. I never quite felt comfortable getting all the praise, so I always made sure I went a step further by returning a compliment. I really enjoy showering love and acceptance to all who crossed my path, and as I have mentioned before, that is my message. I was taught to lead by example, and I know that once the mind gets on track, the body has no choice but to follow.

THE GODDESS LEAGUE

3

THE BODY

POSTURE. GRACE. ELEGANCE. Each of these attributes can be used in describing how you want your body to be conveyed. Your demeanor can speak volumes about your character, without most knowing the wiser. People will treat you accordingly, and it is all based on how you carry yourself. It is your vessel, protect, love and nurture it. Own who you are, because God doesn't make mistakes.

Demeanor equates attitude. For some, that can either be cast in a positive or negative light. Unfortunately, it can be swayed in both directions, but you will learn that there is not much you can do about that. Take each lesson as it comes, so you can add to your arsenal or collection of tools on how to react when/if that particular situation arises. In my case, when my demeanor was concerned, some would say, "You think you all that." Quite the contrary! I suppose I always wanted to convey that I looked better than I felt. I was always surprised when people would say such things.

My response would be "Well, not really, but you must think I am, so thank you!" This goes back to my taking insults as a compliment and letting it roll off my back. I just assumed they didn't know any better, so I had to be the bigger person. Now, the way I carried myself suggested otherwise, and I always had an assurance about myself that made people notice. Some people would stop mid conversation with their mouth gaping open, and I was always tempted to go and close it for them! However, you are aware of the word boundaries? Well, so am I and I respected them! Still, I wasn't aware of the effect I was having on people, and all I was doing was merely walking or standing. Sheesh! You would think that I was standing on my head while juggling balls with my feet the way they would gawk! I started to understand that people felt the way in which I carried myself was based on my perception of who I was. When I looked at it that way, then I had to agree. Yeah, you could say I was all that, and it sounded so much better coming from someone else rather than myself. Again, that was all portrayed without one word from me. Leave an impression!

 Posture. Posture is my favorite subject because when you walk with confidence with your head held high, it can reflect a sort of majestic vibe. People will tend to sit up a little straighter and put you in an entirely different category. You send a message of someone to be respected and admired. People are going to look at you as a tall Goddess in awe. I say if they are going to look, let's give them something to stare at! I know everyone reading this isn't going to have that attitude. I had come to realize that no matter how much I tried to downplay who I was, it only created MORE attention. So, I say, "own it." No matter how you may wish that you were born shorter, the harsh truth is that you were not. So you must ask yourself what you are going to do with such a precious and rare gift? You strut, baby. Strut like a peacock and have them wishing they were you! My strut/walk was a work in progress. As I mentioned before, I wasn't very coordinated, and I could barely walk and chew gum at the same time. Since I knew that and was tired of embarrassing fiascos, I looked into modeling. I didn't get into it heavily until I moved to Atlanta, Georgia in my early twenties. My older sisters kind of had my interest piqued. They would model these beautiful bridal gowns, and I remember thinking: Wow, they are so poised, graceful and majestic. Yes, I talked like that in my head at twelve years old!

You must remember my nose was always in a book, so my vocabulary was crazy good! Anyways, I wanted to be just like them, but it was not meant to be at the time. I wanted to join them on the runway, but I was too skinny and too tall to properly fill out the dresses. Having that goal gave me a sense of pride that I would eventually be able to do what they were doing, and it was only a matter of time.

I want you to know that you should never feel ashamed of who you are, especially when you have no say so in the matter, particularly concerning your genetics. There is absolutely nothing we can do to camouflage height, so you shouldn't sacrifice your posture trying to make others feel comfortable or by trying to make yourself "fit in." While everyone is trying to come up with ways of standing out and being different, we are already equipped with being memorable just by being born! Crazy to think about it that way, right? I know, but seriously, it is the absolute truth. As I mentioned, I went through an awkward growth phase when I was uncoordinated, but that was due to not having body awareness. In simple terms, my brain and body did not function as one. It's almost like I could feel when my space was being breached, and I had to adjust so

I wouldn't make a fool of myself nearly as frequently. Imagine driving a car if you would. This analogy may go over the heads of the ones that can't drive yet, but bear with me. You know your car is a certain size, so with that information you can maneuver it accordingly. You wouldn't park it in places that were too small nor would you drive it under a bridge that was too low. This is how I imagined my body. It was like I was in traffic and had to bob and weave without getting hit or hitting anybody. Instinctively, I would know which doorways I would need to duck to get into or when boarding planes which height heels I could get away with wearing. Yes, I wear heels quite frequently, but I will get to that in a minute.

 I wanted to share with you about a time when I joined the United States Air Force. I only made it to the 5th week of boot camp. Let me say between being a soldier and modeling, I really started to come into my own. If you knew me then, you knew how girly I was, so I shocked many people when they learned that I was a soldier in training. Even to me, it sounded crazy. During my time at boot camp, I had two drill sergeants. One was a woman, and the other a man. They were constantly on my case. I had joined in January, so it was cold in San Antonio, and we would have to get up at four a.m., just because they were there to make our lives miserable. I remember thinking from the time they herded us off that bus on the first night, what have I gotten myself into? We would have to wake up to trumpets every morning and hustle to get our sweatsuits on, just to rush into an open pavilion, and line up and sing Wild Blue Yonder; the official song of the Air Force. We would then proceed to the Mess Hall for breakfast. I never had an appetite. I was so scared in the beginning. All of my unit would cry ourselves to sleep every night for the first couple of days, because it was so much harder than we had anticipated. It ended up being the best experience of my life. While I was there, I was given the distinct privilege of being named Flight Guideon (pronounced Guide-on), and I had the responsibility of carrying my unit flag every time my flight marched anywhere on base. It was not exactly a leadership position because I didn't have the authority to tell people what to do, but it was still a very important position nonetheless. I still told them what to do, even though that wasn't a part of my job description! I knew that I could bear the responsibility and exude leadership qualities. I got that position mainly because I was the tallest one in my squad and the easiest to spot during a march if we were to get split up. That flag was attached to the heaviest pole, so I had to build my stamina up because my arm was exhausted. I remember always getting reprimanded on my strides being too long and to stop switching my hips so much. Let me tell you that it was not an easy feat! I told you I was "girlie," and I didn't even know I was doing it! Apparently, I was leaving behind my squad, and that was unacceptable, not to mention I wasn't marching like a soldier either. I was just all wrong for the job, but I was determined. Over the few short weeks I was there, I learned discipline, had a ridiculous physical work ethic and just overall blossomed. I was groomed to become a better woman, and I was really digging it. Unfortunately, I was one week away from graduation, and my heart decided to act up. I had a pre-existing heart condition called Supraventricular Tachycardia, in short, SVT, and I was discharged. I was so sad because I felt like I had finally found my place, but that was not to be. It had served its purpose. A year later, I ended up getting an opportunity of a lifetime with American Idol. So, I said all that to say this: Circumstances will shape your growth, so there is not a quick way to become your ultimate persona.

I know that experience was vital to understanding my circumference of motion. I left the military not nearly as clumsy, and I was in great physical shape. I couldn't believe the change I made in five weeks, because I started to walk a little more gracefully, and people started to comment. I wanted to hone in on that particular new asset, because I liked the way it made me feel. I like to believe I always had good posture; I never slouched in a chair or walked like I had a hump on my back. However, when I returned home, you could say I was more refined, and I walked a little taller with my head held high.

Elegance would eventually be introduced and heels became my best friend. I felt beautiful, poised, powerful and classy. The heels gave me a sturdier feel; I seemed to walk with purpose, not to mention they made my legs look great! I never once shied away from heels, and the taller heels were the better. I don't know why, but I liked the view better. I could see everything and everyone! I would be lying if I said I liked the attention. I did tend to get looked at as a sideshow freak; children and adults would want a picture with me. If you are ever wondering what a day in the life of a celebrity would be like, just take a page from your everyday life as a Goddess.

Lucky for me I did get to experience being a semi-celebrity for a short while, and I guess you could say I was already groomed for such an experience. In 2007, I auditioned for American Idol and made the top forty. I was on national TV for the first time in my life and what a ride! I had only decided to audition after failing to place in a local talent show. The prize was a paid round trip flight to Seattle and the guarantee to skip the line. I wanted to go and audition, so I raised the money for a flight ticket. I managed just enough to pay the cab fare with an extra fifty dollars to spare. I didn't know where I was going to sleep that night; all I knew was that as long as I went, God would take care of me. I kid you not, the moment I stepped foot out of the cab, another one was pulling up behind me. This girl got out of the cab, and we started chatting. I told her I didn't know where I was going to stay, and she told me she had an extra bed in her hotel and would only charge me fifty dollars if I wanted to stay. I cried and shouted for joy! That was how I KNEW I was right where I was supposed to be, and I couldn't thank God enough for rewarding me for walking by faith and not by sight. This was a blessing indeed!

Now, let me give you a little back story on Idol. As many people have probably figured out by now, so much of it is edited for our viewing pleasure. First and foremost, the terrible singers weren't getting a chance to just waltz in and sing for Simon, Paula and Randy just because they waited in line. OH NO! They were getting hand selected by producers to spice up the show. There were over twenty thousand singers in attendance in Seattle and only forty-five of us made the cut to meet the judges. That included the good and the bad. It was a brutal process and one that I wouldn't recommend to anyone, because they try to tear you apart mentally. If you are not made with durability, then it was off with your head. I had made sure to wear my heels, because as I told you, they gave me confidence and stability. After I got my yellow ticket to proceed to the Hollywood rounds, I watched it back on TV Simon said: "I think she is the tallest lady I have ever seen." He proceeded to call me a giraffe, but he apologized for it later. I told him not to worry about it, because his cruelty made me famous. He told me that he wished everyone could handle his critiques so elegantly. He is actually a nice man, and I enjoyed the little time I was able to spend around him.

At the time, I didn't know the effect choosing to wear high heels would have on the public. The day after my audition aired, my Facebook inbox was flooded, and I got hundreds upon hundreds of friend requests. I soon found out the reach that I had. The messages I received were mainly from tall women, who were inspired by me having worn heels. They too were finally finding the courage to put on a pair of heels. Some were in their forties; others were young women. I even had a few kids inbox me to say that I made them feel like they weren't alone. I made them feel normal. These women, over forty, told me that because of me they felt the freedom to wear heels for the first time in their lives! I remember receiving pictures because they wanted to share with me how happy they were when wearing heels for the first time. I was floored and humbled to think that a girl who came from a small town and was only twenty years old could have such an impact. It was a heck of a welcoming, and I was moved to tears, because I thought everyone embraced their height. I simply didn't know any other way to be. I had a Mom who was over six feet tall and siblings who stood above the rest. They dressed with their own style and they were very fashionable. They have always stood out from all others. I have always done what felt natural, and I didn't conform to the opinions of society on how I should look or dress. Many times people had the audacity to ask me why I wore heels because they felt as though I was tall enough. I would respond by saying "short people aren't limited to only wearing heels, right?" Lord knows, it would've been most helpful if only I could have seen them coming! So why should I only be limited to wearing flats? It didn't and still doesn't make sense to me. I am a woman, and I want to embody everything that comes with it, because that is my right. During my fifteen minutes of fame, I was taking pictures and holding babies just like the President! (NO kissing the babies though, nuh-uh!) As I told you, I was already getting a small taste of attention just by being tall, so I suppose you could say I fell into the role with ease. I remember getting my picture published on the front page of the local newspaper, and the sense of awe and wonder that everyone was so proud of me was very exhilarating!

Sometimes, I had to get my mind right. When I would step out in public, I couldn't "go off" on people

when they decided to satisfy their curiosity concerning my height. I already knew the questions I would be asked. Everyone wanted to know my height and if I played basketball. I also knew those questions would follow me for the rest of my life. I had two options. I could either learn to accept the questions or choose to walk around with a bad attitude. I would much rather be in a good mood, because it takes way less effort, and it's contagious. It is wise to know your patience and your limits so you don't lose your sanity trying to always be cordial. Some people don't know when to quit, and once you get them going, they will hold you amidst interrogation for the rest of the night. They would say things like "I was pretty for a tall girl, or "I bet you I can beat you in a game of one on one." I was NEVER good at one on one, and I learned to overlook the other nonsense. What am I supposed to say? I feel compelled to tell you that it takes great patience to not respond with sarcasm! In those moments, you have to know when your patience limit has been met. Maturity is learning to walk away from people and situations that threaten your peace of mind, self-respect, morals and self-worth. I learned to politely excuse myself and to keep it moving.

When you think of the body, I think of the image I want to create. Complimentary clothing goes a long way, because certain articles of clothing flatter us better than others. One of my main concerns upon talking to tall girls in middle and high school was the fact that they had nothing to wear. It wasn't that they had nothing to wear; they just didn't have the knowledge on where to shop or what would look good on them. Most of them would dress in sweats and oversized tees, because it was the most comfortable and required the least effort. Sneakers were a staple piece in their wardrobe, along with hoodies and jogger pants. Now, I am all for comfortability, but some of these young women never knew what they looked like in clothes that fit. I found that fact to be disheartening and troublesome, because no one had ever taken the time to introduce them to different options. Thankfully, in this day and age, there are more options than ever for us, because the world is finally catching up. I think many of us tend to go wrong, my prior self included, when we wear something we saw our friends wearing. However, this doesn't apply to all of my readers. Speaking from a personal standpoint, that T-shirt dress is going to look like an actual T-Shirt on us, and those booty shorts are going to look like a thong. Those baby doll tees are going to appear as a sports bra! If I do say so myself, these don't make the best looks for us. I have always been a fan of kimonos and dusters. I love the way they drape on a long frame and how cute they make me feel. They give me so much LIFE, dahlin'!!!

As a woman of height, I think it is important to feel this way and clothing plays a huge part in that.

The ability to balance how you look and feel makes the haters and spectators more in awe, because we are unicorns…rare and magical. Own every ounce of yourself! If you find things about yourself you want to change, try and find your happy medium. I am not saying this will happen overnight, but instead of focusing on all our imperfections, we should shift the attention to what we like. Since our bodies are the first thing people see, it is usually what we most desire to change.

THE GODDESS LEAGUE

4

HARMONY

THE UNITY OF the mind, body and spirit is something sought after but not easily achieved. Our spirit is the core of where our sense of self is revealed at its purest form. Our actions and thoughts are the way we express ourselves. You will find that the universe will reward you when the mind, body and spirit are on one accord. I must reemphasize that I had to acquire the skill of shutting down negativity, and it was because I wanted to keep joy in my spirit. Let me expand on that: joy is an elevated sense of happiness, a surety of oneself. It can only come when you make peace with not only who you are but why you are and how you are. Whereas, happiness tends to be externally triggered and is based on other people, things, places, thoughts and events. It is extremely hard to keep me down, because no matter how good or bad life is, I still choose to wake up each morning and be thankful there is still one to have. Someone who is no longer in the land of the living understands too late the essence of feeling AT ALL. You see, feeling something negative means that you are ALIVE and breathing, and it is up to you to either succumb to that treacherous state of momentary disregard or find joy and meaning within you. Begin today, by using a different approach to what you take with you to avoid breathing life into the negativity of others. If you can leave it where it is, then you are already on the right path. So many of the chapters in my book can be tied together, because my message goes back to your mind. If you have a solid structure of who you are, then the words of people who try to disintegrate or tear apart the structure you have built will be impenetrable. I found that I was like a magnet to people, not only for my boundless confidence, but because my light radiated to all those around me. I loved to feed people positive energy, and I had stored enough of it to go around. Everything always reverts back to my personal mission of spreading love and acceptance to all that cross my path. I want each of you to feel as though you are special and that you are worthy.

    I am not saying that you have to go to this extent, but I am merely letting you know what I felt my purpose was and still is. Every time I acted on it, I would feel a sense of gratitude that I was fulfilling my destiny. I loved that feeling! A couple of years ago, I had the opportunity to be a host for this online publication. I was given access to multiple concerts and even got to attend Essence Fest in New Orleans. First and foremost, the camera and I have always been friends. I don't shy away from it, not to mention my delight in talking to anyone that will listen. It was a perfect job for me! I grew up knowing that my passions were reading, writing and talking so I knew that Journalism was the path I was supposed to take. I didn't know which job I would have but I knew it would have to entail one of the three. I said that to say I found people coming up to me asking if they could be interviewed by me (which I was surprised by because they didn't even know or care what it was for they just saw me with a microphone) and I think being approachable played a major part in them feeling comfortable to do so. I always wanted to be as cheerful as possible because the world can be so full of the opposite. Having the opportunity to touch people on a bigger platform was an honor but a responsibility as well. I relished being spontaneous and thinking on my feet and walking up to strangers wanting to know their thought and opinions on certain topics but it was also pressure. Pressure to always be on because I knew

I had the spotlight and didn't want to mess up. What I want you to take from this is it is ok to be honest with yourself. It is ok to admit fear of failure or be aware of your shortcomings. Stop trying to be something or someone you are not. Truly I never wanted to be around someone who "appeared" to have it all together because I couldn't relate nor did I feel as though they were genuinely likeable. I always respected and admired the ones who could openly admit the struggle is real. I am my biggest critic and biggest supporter. I know the things I should improve on and do my best to apply that accordingly. That is why I stressed having a mentor to be so important because we should always seek out someone that can remove themselves from the situation and see it for what it is. I was constantly trying to be someone I was not. I thought that if I looked and sounded a certain way that I would be accepted. Often times I would send out the wrong signals in reference to my personality and had to work overtime to get it back on the right track. For example sometimes it can take me a little while to warm up to someone and automatically I am considered hostile. It was so frustrating because I always felt if it were coming from someone else I wouldn't be labeled as such. In that respect I would then try and make them see the light of just how awesome I am! That goes back to me trying to please everyone and gaining no traction. You will find yourself in a sort of limbo and that does no good to your psyche. I always sought out effective communication but it seemed some people were going to continue to think the way they wanted and I had to either let that go or shoulder the weight and responsibility of trying to prove otherwise.

    I couldn't live in harmony that way and it took me awhile to balance it all out. I am programmed to always try and see the best in people so if/when they fell short I had to stop personally feeling affected. Sometimes the energy you give off isn't going to immediately trickle down. That is where being consistently confident in the person you are will come into play and the effect will be profound. Patience is the name of the game and sometimes all it takes is a little reminder. Often times people are going to get the wrong impression of us and it is up to us to change the perspective.

    I was recently taking a stroll and saw another tall lady. I proceeded to give her a compliment. I always love when I see another tall woman. I want them to know that they rock and to remind them of how gorgeous they are. Now this is probably the southern roots in me, so I know for a fact that everyone reading this won't be as comfortable doing so and that is ok! I am not telling you to do this, I am just sharing my story… so she chose to ignore me. It was almost as if she could not fathom me of all people giving her a compliment! It is like we were supposed to just act like the other doesn't exist. I am sorry, but I am not programmed that way. On another occasion I was at a mixer and it was filled with many high profile people. I wasn't the only tall Goddess in attendance (naturally). So when I spotted another tall beauty I made my way over to her. She was very pleasant but seemed surprised. I made sure to introduce myself and told her we were kindred sisters in height. I wanted her to know that she looked amazing and she was polite enough to say the same things back. I then gave her a hug and parted ways. Mind you when I give hugs, it's not the one arm pat, church hugs, because I like to really let you feel my sincerity. I wrap both arms tightly around you while I squeeze! I don't believe she was ready for the whole exchange. I then gave her my card, because I wanted us to keep in touch. I must admit I do love having tall beautiful, warm friends, not to mention uplifting, supportive and

encouraging. I am very fortunate to always be in the company of such beings as I have girlfriends that are a great extension of myself. Needless to say I never heard from her which didn't necessarily surprise me, because I could tell that was not who she is and I might have made her uncomfortable in the long run. I would like to say we are not each others' competition. She may have been used to the idea of being the tallest person in the room and taking all the attention. I am really not sure. This is an assumption but I think she wanted to dislike me because I was threatening those very things unbeknownst to me. She couldn't dislike me, because I wanted her to feel beautiful and I told her as much. You see the lesson to be learned here is that you must kill people with so much kindness that they feel foolish for ever thinking differently of you in the first place. They are only going to regurgitate what you gave to them back to you. I have nothing bad to say about the young lady as I only made an observation.

The message in this chapter is to find ways to be in harmony with yourself and live your best life. I didn't do what was expected of me because again I don't live by societal standards. I am sure some people would have loved for us to talk crap about the other just to give them some tea to spill, giving them something to gossip about. I refused to give them the satisfaction. I don't care if I never see anyone act the way that I do, because I do what is right and what makes me feel good. I am not naïve enough to think everyone will practice such ways but one can hope! I feel like if a person is unfortunate enough to not have anyone to lift them up, then you should be the missing link and fill the gap. I just want to always acknowledge another Goddess and express my joy at finding such rare and magical unicorns.

With that I would like to leave you with encouragement to take care of yourself and try to be mindful of your health. Selective foods, exercise and daily intake of water is what fuels the body and keeps us looking good. That is what we all desire right? Thankfully we live in a day and age where all body types are celebrated and being one certain way is no longer. I know for me personally I couldn't WAIT for the day I would weigh in

at two hundred pounds only to find out the scale can and will go higher! I stress staying healthy because as tall women we neglect that part and it is because we have so many places for the pounds to go so we can disguise it well. Love you and all parts of you because you only live once. So let us put our best foot forward and start making the most of it shall we?

Join me in sharing your story because it starts with YOU.

"Our deepest fear is not that we are inadequate. Our deepest fear is that we are powerful beyond measure. It is our light, not our darkness that most frightens us. We ask ourselves, "Who am I to be brilliant, gorgeous, talented and fabulous?" Actually, who are you not to be?

YOU ARE A CHILD OF GOD. Your playing small does not serve the world. This is nothing enlightened about shrinking so that other people won't feel insecure around you. We were born to manifest the glory that is within us. As we let our light shine, we unconsciously give other people permission to do the same.

Epilogue

HELP. COMPASSION. CONFIDENCE. HOPE.

It has been my desire that the words offered in the pages of this book, have helped you to find the purest part of yourself. The goal here is to remind you that you are beautiful inside as well as out. When referencing your height and all of the obstacles that will come along with it, you should feel a sense of pride. Let that pride surge through you and it will spill abundantly to touch those around you! All of your challenges are not in vain. They will shape you into who you are destined to become…Yes, we will be tested but isn't the reward greater than the risk? Be bold, be beautiful, be confident, but most of all be better than you were yesterday.

Loved the book? I would enjoy your feedback! Be sure to like my Facebook Page: www.facebook.com/

www.ingramcontent.com/pod-product-compliance
Lightning Source LLC
Chambersburg PA
CBHW060343080526
44584CB00013B/893